THE POETRY OF WALLACE STEVENS

A Note on the Type

This book was set on the Linotype in Century Expanded, designed in 1894 by Linn Boyd Benton (1844–1932). Benton cut Century Expanded in response to Theodore De Vinne's request for an attractive, easy-to-read typeface to fit the narrow columns of his *Century Magazine*. Early in the nineteen hundreds Morris Fuller Benton updated and improved Century in several versions for his father's American Type Founders Company. Century remains the only American typeface cut before 1910 still widely in use today.

Composed by Maryland Linotype Composition Company, Baltimore, Maryland. Printed and bound by The Haddon Craftsmen, Scranton, Pennsylvania. Typography and binding design by Virginia Tan.